Old Things

Written by **Adrian Bell**

Fast phonics

Before reading this book, ask the student to practise saying the sounds (phonemes) and reading the new words used in the book. Try to make it as speedy and as fun as possible.

Read the tricky high frequency words

The student can't sound out these words at the moment, but they need to know them because they are commonly used.

| their | here |

Tip: Encourage the student to sound out any sounds they know in these words, and you can provide them with the irregular or tricky part.

Say the sounds

ow	o	oa	ea
snow	yo-yo	boat	beach
e	y	ay	a
me	jelly	play	paper
a-e	y	i-e	i
plane	cry	bike	lion

Tip: Remember to say the pure sounds. For example, 'ssss' and 'nnnn'. If you need a reminder, watch the *Snappy Sounds* videos.

Snappy words

Point at a word randomly and have the student read the word. The student will need to sound out the word and blend the sounds to read the word. For example: 'f–o–ll–ow, follow'.

show	<u>ago</u>	dino
grow	follow	window
slow	grown	<u>below</u>
throw	go	going
most	post	own
blow	yellow	won't
don't	pillow	no

Quick vocabulary check

The underlined words may not be familiar to the student. Check their understanding before you start to read the book.

We are on a trip to see old things.

Old things can show us what life was like long ago.

Follow us as we show you lots of old things. We will go slow, so you won't get lost.

This display shows an old bedroom with no **power**.

window

pillow

Long ago, it was colder and darker inside. We won't find heaters or lights here.

This display shows an old kitchen.

a loaf for making toast

Long ago, most people had to roast and boil their food on a coal fire. This old cooker was slow.

This display shows an old boat with sails.

Long ago, there were no cars. Old boats took people and things from **coast** to coast.

coach

This display shows us what life was like when we didn't have cars.

Some people went by **coach**, but it was very slow. Horses towed them down the road. This coach took the post, too.

This display shows a man hunting for food. Don't go too near the spear!

A long time ago, people had to throw **spears** and blow darts to catch their own food. They may have grown food, too.

This display shows us what very old art was like.

yellow paint

Long ago, people lived in caves. They liked to show their paintings inside their caves.

A very long time ago, there were different living things, such as dinos.

This display shows us the size of a big dino!

We can look at a dino from below!

How big did dinos grow?

They were big and little sizes.

Old things from long ago make us think.

Old things show us how people and things grow over time.

Glossary

coach   a kind of cart towed by horses

coast   the land next to the sea

power   how people get light and heat

spears   tools with sharp points for going hunting

Comprehension questions

Well done!

Let's talk about the story together

Ask the student:
- What did you learn about old things?
- What did the coach need to make it move?
- Can you find the word that is short for 'dinosaur'?
- What old things would you like to learn about? Why? How will you find information about them?

Snappy words

Ask the student to read these words as quickly as they can.

ago	follow	window
slow	grown	below
dino	going	show

Fluency

Can the student read the story again and improve on the last time?

Have fun!